LOVE HER

By

OSCAR JONES

Cover by Kingdom Graphic Designs

Edited, formatted and published by

Destiny House Publishing, LLC.

P.O. Box 19774

Detroit, MI 48219

404.993.0830

www.destinyhousepublishing.com

email: inquiry@destinyhousepublishing.com

Cover Design by Kingdom Graphic Designs

ISBN: 978-1-936867-57-8

CONTENTS

ACKNOWLEDGMENTS

I want to thank God for His amazing work in my life. Because of His Love towards me, it has allowed me to become the man that I am.

To my bride, my one flesh partner, Crystal Jones, I am grateful to God for your love and respect towards me. You are incredible and I thank you for the love and respect in our marriage.

I also thank you for the work that you did to help me publish this book

Chapter 1
IS LOVE ENOUGH?

———————○○———————

Has your wife ever complained that you don't love her? If so, don't despair. Most men have heard the 'unloved' accusation at one time or another in their marriage. And it doesn't seem very encouraging because to us, it feels like she doesn't value our love. She does not appreciate the day-to-day grind of going to work and providing for your household. You do it for the love of your God and family. However, when you hear the allegation of lovelessness, it stings. And it seems that what you do doesn't count.

You figure that the two of you are doing life together. You both bring something to the table. You pay bills, help around the house, mow the lawn, discipline the children, and a host of other things that she minimizes. If you were to bring it up, she would say that's what you are supposed to do. You know deep down it's true, but you still want credit for it. I get it.

But what if instead of looking at how your wife responds to your love, you looked at how God says we should love her. Just perhaps the way that we love her is insufficient.

Every woman yearns to be loved and adored by her husband. She wants to be thought of as special in his eyes. She wants to know that he is willing to give up everything for her.

Christ's bride is special and favored. He gave up everything for her. Ephesians 5:25 says it is our duty to love our wives like Christ loved the church. It is God's command. We are to love them, nourish them, cherish them, and take care of them.

But if we really want to learn how to love our wives, we must be willing to humble ourselves. Pride will keep us stuck at one level. But God promises that He can do exceeding above all that we can ask or imagine. So that means there is always room in our marriages for improvement and growth.

If we are willing, God will teach us. The best way is to learn from his example. Christ loved His bride, the church. Even though she mocked him, spit upon him, and beat him to death, he still looked at her with love and compassion in his eyes and asked the Father to forgive her. Our Loving Lord doesn't hold grudges. He forgives. He doesn't mistreat his bride, neglect her or try to control her. He keeps her 'free will" intact. He loves her in spite of her complaints and ungrateful spirit. His love is so strong that it covers her sins.

God's love is lavish. He offers it to us and then expects us to receive it for ourselves and then turn around and offer this same love to our wives. A new commandment I give unto you, that you love one another; as I have loved you, that ye also love one another. (John 13:34 KJV)

This love is passionate, intense, and readily available. It's not measured by whether we perform some duty or obligation. Neither does it hinge on how we conduct ourselves. It knows no limits, it is bold, and it is a love without question.

As men, we generally don't express love to our wives like that. And yet we struggle to understand why our "ordinary" love is not enough. Let me help you. Think about how we love things, and we can easily see how we come up short.

We love cars, sports, or other hobbies. We spend so much of our money, time and energy to give attention to those things. Some men will sit in a stadium in 10 below zero weather because of their love for football. Others deck themselves out in their favorite team's gear and watch for hours on end from their sofas. Car fanatics will spend more than their fair share on restoring some vintage vehicle and attending various car shows. Ultimately, we invest, time and money in what we love.

But what do you do to express the love you have for your wife? How have you invested in her? Is your love undeniable? Are you willing to sacrifice for her? Answer honestly. It's the only way to grow.

When you measure your love for her by your willingness to go to work and earn a paycheck, your love will seem to come up a little short. You go to work and involve yourself in the other things that you love and still those areas get more. It's no wonder, she feels neglected.

Your wife wants to be adored by you. She wants to feel special. It is important that you make the intentional effort of expressing your love to her in passionate ways. The passion of Christ is his bride. We see it all through the scriptures. Is your bride your passion? It's the only way to ensure that your love is enough. Go beyond ordinary and show her extraordinary love.

Chapter 2
GIVING YOURSELF

C hrist was so passionate about his bride, that he was willing to give himself up for her. He was faultless, and she was flawed, but He couldn't stomach the thought of her taking the punishment that she rightly deserved, so he took her place. He became her substitution and laid down His life so that she could live. It's the most beautiful love story in the world. This is a selfless love, agape love.

It does not come easy for us, because we are born selfish by nature. From a child, we have been self-serving. It's all about 'me' and 'mine'. Learning to become selfless is a spiritual concept and a confrontation with our flesh. The flesh wants its way. To assassinate the flesh, we must live in the presence of God.

Giving of ourselves consistently is hard work but a work that must be done. Christ commands us as husbands to give ourselves as he gave himself for the church. Jesus is the bridegroom and a perfect role model for all of us. Giving of myself requires that I put my wife's needs ahead of my own. As her leader, I seek to serve her and make sure she has what is needed.

My love covers her. It also means that I will never intentionally throw her under the bus in any situation or circumstance. Nor do I take potshots or make jokes at her expense. I am her protector. I must properly steward my care for her.

I have not always covered my wife as I should have. Earlier in our marriage, there were times when my family members and some of her family members would disrespect her, talk about her and I wouldn't say anything. In my silence, I was protecting myself, and I was leaving her out there to be attacked. I was more concerned with how I looked or what others thought about me. I left her uncovered.

Learning how to cover your spouse is about protecting her from the insults and attacks from others. A leader has to protect his family from all assaults, even when he doesn't feel like he can and when he may be nervous because he doesn't like confrontation. The responsibility still falls upon his shoulders, as the head of the family. No matter what our personalities, to be an effective leader, we must step up to protect our wives. Your children are watching and learning from the script you hand them. Your sons will learn to follow your example, and your daughters will learn what to expect from a husband. A leader must stand in the gap for those he leads.

It is not enough to love your wife sexually and bring in financial support. There is so much more to being a husband than that. If I really love her, I must give my total self to her (mind, will, and emotions).

In marriage, we start far from where we will end up. Thank God there is grace to grow. We will evolve as husbands if we choose to. So we may start out protecting ourselves over protecting our wives. But that's not where we will end up. We must *intentionally* grow from this place. God's love requests that we purposely put our brides ahead of ourselves, suffering on her behalf. By giving myself for her, I show how much she means to me.

There are many times in our lives that we will have the opportunity to cover them. And we must step up to the plate, no matter what it costs us. There are some battles that she will have to fight for herself, and God will cover her. But when it's on us, we must be men and deal with the enemy. God has given us the ability to cover her. So when there is an opportunity to protect her or yourself, choose her. Lay down your life for hers.

Often, we are guilty of withholding a part of ourselves from our wives. It's the vulnerable part of ourselves that we tuck neatly away from female eyes. We are afraid of her judgment, her criticism, and her rejection. And so we shield this part of ourselves; not realizing it distances us from her. Many times we hide emotionally, not wanting to confront the issues that nag at us to take action. I admit it's not easy. But it is certainly possible. We must strive to emotionally connect with ourselves so that we can connect with our wives.

Certainly, you can't expose your vulnerable places to your wife before she is mature enough to handle it. She, too, has to grow. Where she is currently - is not where she will end. So, you must be willing to be vulnerable. Maybe it's not for this season, but keep trying in another season. There are incredible rewards to reap when you completely trust your wife. Your marriage will go to heights you never imagined.

The heart of her husband doth safely trust in her, so that he shall have no need of spoil. (Proverbs 31:11 KJV)

I am in this season of my marriage where I can literally tell my wife anything. She has my back and keeps my confidences. She doesn't use my vulnerabilities against me, and I know that she is on my side. Of course, we didn't start here. We both grew to this place. It took years.

My relationship with God helped me to grow in this place. It is the catalyst for all other growth. We must be an example of godliness to our families. I know the church tends to expect more spirituality from the wives. Even some wives believe themselves to be the spiritual leaders of their homes. This is not biblical.

The husband is the head and leader of the home.. Ephesian 5:23a says For the husband is the head of the wife, even as Christ is the head of the Church. And so it is incumbent upon the men to find their place in God to be able to properly lead their families. Develop your own prayer life and study of the Word. Again, there is space to grow. So you may start out praying for five minutes a day. That's fine. You may only read one or two verses. But if you are consistent, you won't stay there. But it's a wonderful starting place. And you will find yourself enjoying God's presence.

Don't neglect time in the word and prayer or leave that "duty" to your wife. If you are going to lead, you must be able to know where you are going. Without a relationship with the Lord, you lead blindly. You can't expect from your family what you aren't willing to do.

I have not always led my wife properly in the marriage. Which may give you an understanding of why earlier on in the marriage, I didn't cover her as I should. I had to learn how to lead her and pray for her spiritually. But all of this comes in my relationship with Christ; as I give myself to him, He, in turn, teaches me and shows me how to lead her. The Holy Spirit will guide us if we let him. Our relationship with Him will be developed over our lifetimes. So don't get discouraged where you are right now, ask the Holy Spirit to lead you and he will teach you how to lead your wife.

In essence, we must give ourselves to the Lord before we can give ourselves up for her.

The average husband tends to work hard to provide for the family. He works to meet the sexual needs of his wife. He may help around the house and do repairs. However, the more profound work is in the emotional and spiritual realms. That's the difference between an average husband and an amazing husband.

I have been married for 38 years and there have been times that I have disconnected from my spouse, emotionally. Those times came because I was struggling with my own emotions. And sometimes I couldn't reconcile what it was. As men, we must find an outlet, another man to talk and share with. As we find that connection on a personal level, we will begin to connect better with our wives.

We are all emotional beings. Our wives tend to live with their emotions in a deeper sense. That does not make them weird or inferior. It's just the way women are wired. She needs your connection, just like we must be connected to Christ. Think about your connection with Christ and how you feel when you are one with Him. The communion you feel with being in connection with your Lord energizes you. It causes you to believe His word. In the same way, your wife needs that connection with you.

LOVE HER

Chapter 3
DOES SHE DESERVE IT?

If your wife is still growing into maturity, you might not feel like she deserves your love. Maybe she's loud or disrespectful. Perhaps she is controlling or bitter. Whether or not you feel as if your wife deserves it or has "earned" it, you are called to love her without condition.

Some men complain that their wives are disrespectful, and they want their honor before they are willing to love them. But God told us to copy Him, love her like He loves his bride. While we were yet sinners, Christ died for us. He didn't wait until we got it together. God didn't wait for us to respect him before he would offer himself as a sacrifice on our behalf. Nope. He died first. In fact, right smack in the midst of the church disrespecting Him, he chose to love her to death. She mocked him, spit on him. Guards were gambling for his clothing. He received no honor whatsoever. Still, …he decided to go to the cross in her place. And that's the way we have got to approach loving our wives.

It's striking how we can love our children no matter what they do or how immature or rebellious they act. We don't withhold love from them. They may receive more discipline, but the love we have never diminishes.

What does the Word say? Let's look at Ephesians 5. Husbands, love your wives, just as Christ also loved the church and gave Himself up for her (26) so that he might sanctify her, having cleansed her by the washing of water with the word., (27) that he may present to Himself the church in all her glory, having no spot or wrinkle or any such thing, but that she would be holy and blameless. (28) So husbands are also to love their own wives as their own bodies.. He who loves his wife loves himself. (29) for no one ever hated his own flesh, but he nourishes and cherishes it, just as Christ also does the church. (Ephesians 5:25-29 NASB)

Do you take good care of yourself? Well according to the word, you are to care for your wife's financial, emotional, physical needs and desires in the same way that you take care of your own. She is not to be neglected. Love her above your work, your hobbies, friends, and your other family members (including your mom!) – choose your wife first.

The scripture says no man hates his own body but loves it and nourishes it. The same way you give attention to yourself and your interests, you ought to do the same for your wife.

Think about how Christ won us over. He loved us first. Our attention was not even turned toward Him. While we were living our lives as reckless as possible, He decided to show us, love. And not just a passive love like 'I love watching that show' or 'I love eating some food item.' This type of generic love is passive and requires nothing of you. God expressed agape love which is pure and unlimited. It is expressed in action.

But God commendeth his love toward us, in that, while we were yet sinners, Christ died for us. (Romans 5: 8 KJV)

Herein is love, not that we loved God, but that he loved us, and sent his Son *to be* the propitiation for our sins. (I John 4:10 KJV)

And weren't we compelled by that love? Agape love is attractive. It draws others to us. Maybe your wife is hard to live with. Perhaps she is still reeling from wounds from her childhood or some other traumatic event. God says love her. Your love will cover.

Everyone wants to be loved. It's not a matter of do we need to be loved; our wives deserve to be loved. God doesn't give us an option in that. She is due love in the same way that you are due respect. If you are waiting to love her before you give her respect, you are going about it all wrong. God loved us first. The leader leads.

Rendering love only when you determine she deserves it, is wrong and does not constitute agape love. Agape love is the God-type of love. It is conditional.

Think of the things our wives have had to put up with us: Lack of empathy, impatience, anger, our prayerlessness, deceitfulness, harshness, and the list goes on. We can't demand respect in exchange for love. It's just not God's way.

Love her no matter what. Love her because you love God. Let me say, I love my wife. I love spending time with her. I love going on trips with her. I love talking to her. I love taking care of her. It's not a matter of whether she deserves it or not. It is my desire to please her.

Entitlement is a spirit that can make us think our wives don't deserve what we have to give. But why must she deserve the thing that God told us to give to her? We were created to love and be loved. Do we deserve the love that comes from God? It doesn't matter what we think or how we fall short, God's love is there is from everlasting to everlasting.

God never stops loving us no matter what we do. Even if we think we don't deserve His love, it's irrelevant because

God is love. He loves us in spite of ourselves. So just like God's love reaches past all our faults to minister to our needs, that's the love that our wives need from us. She doesn't have to measure up to get it.

LOVE HER

Chapter 4
A GIFT

A godly wife is a gift from God. The Bible tells us that houses and riches *are* the inheritance of fathers: and a prudent wife *is* from the Lord. (Proverbs 19:14 KJV)

Prudence is the ability to govern and discipline oneself for use. It is the skill and good judgment in the use of resources. It is a person who is cautious and circumspect as to danger and risk.

Whoso findeth a wife findeth a good thing, and obtaineth favour of the LORD. (Proverbs 18:22 KJV)

A godly wife is prudent and an incredible blessing. It would do us well to remember that. But not only is she a good thing, but also the word tells us that we will receive favor from God because of her. That's an amazing promise.

Husbands may start off seeing their wives as gifts. But after the honeymoon, in the midst of everyday life and struggles, we forget. Maybe she is insecure, mouthy, curt, or sarcastic. Still, she is a gift. It may be hard to see. But in the middle of the broken exterior is something beautiful and wonderful that God intended for us to have.

It's like the diamonds found in the earth, you will have to dig deep to get the treasure. Your wife isn't all that she will be. She will evolve. But look at her and see her future and the amazing woman of God she will become. Speak life to her and about her.

Life may have hindered her. Maybe the way she was raised makes it hard to see the gem that God created. Or it could be because of the deficiencies in our own masculinity that we find it hard to see. Nevertheless, we must take God at His Word and not underestimate the gift that He has given us.

If we are not careful, the enemy can pollute our minds and corrupt our thoughts against our wives. We should not view our wives as objects who were solely created for our pleasure. She is not just here to satisfy you. She is God's creation with a purpose and a charge to glorify him. There is a part of her that doesn't even belong to you, she is God's daughter first.

Then the Lord God made a woman from the rib he had taken out of the man, and he brought her to the man. Genesis 2:22 NIV

Just as God brought Eve to Adam to present her to him, I understand that my wife is a gift that God has chosen specifically for me.

Let's go back to that good thing that God said that he gave us. If we recognize the gift that she is, it will provoke us to treat her well. When you see something as valuable, you tend to take better care of it and give it special attention.

My wife is a gift to me, emotionally, spiritually, and physically. The gift she brings emotionally helps me in those times when I am low. Because she is a prudent wife, she is able to minister to me. There are times she helps me with the direction in decisions that we make together. Other times her words of affirmation go a long way in encouraging me in my manhood and as a husband. And she physically is my companion and lover. I cherish her. She is my gift from God to help me be a better servant of God. And I must properly steward such a precious gift. I would not be where I am today without God's favor and the blessing of my wife. I'm doing what I'm doing by the grace of God and my wife being by my side. So husbands don't take your gift for granted because your gift was given for your benefit.

Men don't tend to navigate emotions as well as women. Our wives help us to deal with situations from an emotional perspective if we allow them in. It may feel risky but it is worth it.

There was a time in my marriage that I struggled with my identity. My wife helped me through the emotional maze I was going through. She prayed me through and affirmed me and helped me to see things from a different perspective. Your wife can be an incredible, blessing if we tap into that part of her.

If your wife is an intercessor, you have an advantage. Most Christian wives pray for their husbands regularly. Don't underestimate the value of a praying wife. It is significant to have a wife that is so spiritually discerning that she can pick up what the enemy is trying to do and relay that to you as the leader. This allows you to make sound decisions in leading the family. When you listen to her, you encourage the intercessor in her. Don't dismiss her because you are *the head.*

Most of us understand the physical benefits of a wife. We appreciate that sexually she comforts us and brings us pleasure. But she is far more than a sexual being. Sex is great. But that's not all there is to her. She is indeed a gift. So treat her as such.

Chapter 5
LEAD HER

An army of a sheep led by a lion will always defeat
an army of lions led by sheep.
Dr. Myles Munroe

God has chosen men to lead their homes. The ultimate test of your manhood is not what you do on the field or court or even what you claim you did back in the day. It is not your ability to launch a business, grow a ministry or develop a team. The ultimate test of your manhood and your leadership is your home life.

The husband is the head of the wife as Christ is the head of the church. Many scriptures talk about the headship of husbands. Men are to lead their wives. Headship is very important to the order in which God created things. The head leads in a way that governs, causing those that follow to thrive and to reach their fullest potential.

God created Adam first from the dust of the ground and breathed life into him. Afterwards, he brought forth Eve from the rib of Adam.

I was not a good leader at the beginning of our marriage. I remember there were times when my wife and I would have conversations. She would literally tell me, "I need you to lead me." Now I know that is unusual for a wife to ask her husband, especially in today's environment; but my wife did. I didn't understand leadership in the beginning, I had to learn it. I studied and prayed. I made many mistakes, but thanks to the grace of God, He didn't allow those mistakes to ruin my marriage and my family.

Every believer is born again to lead. But we must learn how to lead, and that's where the Holy Spirit comes into play. The Lord taught me how to lead my wife, and even to this day, I am still in the class of leadership, learning how to lead her as she changes and our marriage enters into different seasons. Jesus expects us to lead our wives to him.

All headship must be done by love. So know that love is the catalyst to our headship. So we must lovingly lead her at all times. To lovingly lead your wife is to lead her without manipulation and control. We don't lead her for our own selfish purposes, asking her to do things for us that we wouldn't do. Nor do we violate God's word in our leadership. He will certainly deal with us, if we do.

So I must ask myself these questions daily. What kind of leader am I in my home?" "Do I control or manipulate my wife with anger to get my way or get things done in the house?" If we don't know what it means to lovingly lead her, we can find ourselves in control and manipulation without even realizing it.

As I said before, we are to love her as Christ loves us. We must make the parallel between the two; It is a little easier to see His type of love. Lovingly leading her, puts her first. It causes us to look at our motives and behaviors. It is something that is done intentionally. It is not enough to feel love for our wives. But that feeling must be demonstrated. Love is nothing if there is no action behind it.

Leading her means making hard decisions. It may mean making choices that go against what your wife desires. It is choosing to follow Christ regardless to what she thinks. Because God always wants what's best for us and our families.

When our wives are in disagreement or in opposition to what we feel the Lord is leading us to do, it is in those times that our leadership is most tested. How do we handle that? What do we do to demonstrate love. We should consider our wives and their opinions, but we also know that ultimately what we feel the will of God is what we **must** do.

And you will make mistakes. That's okay. Trust that God already knows that. He has made provision for it.

Your leadership will be based on your manhood. That's why it is so important that we be lovers of God and his word. We can only lead to the level of healing in our manhood.

Some men are passive; therefore, leading becomes very difficult. Some men are overbearing and controlling. And if they are not working on their relationship with God, they will try to bully their wives into submission. Obviously, this is NOT the will of God. Wherever we are in our relationship with God will determine how we lead. Therefore it is critically important that we always work on ourselves to become a better son of God. This will make us better husbands and fathers to the benefit of our families.

I had many issues in my leadership. But I had to grow in my walk with Christ and my love for my wife. And those difficulties stemmed from injuries in my manhood. I didn't really know who I was. I had an image issue. I tried to be more than what I was. And a lot of times, I was very passive in my approach to leadership. I didn't or couldn't make decisions. I was a procrastinator, deceiver and a cheater. You see those areas of my manhood hindered me in my leading. Unless I chose to get healing in those areas, I would have continued to have issues in leading my wife. But thank God that He healed me. I matured, and I grew in my walk with Christ. The Holy Spirit taught me every step of the way how to become a better leader to my wife and my family.

I cannot reiterate enough that we are born leaders, but we must learn how to lead. It is my prayer, men of God, that we learn how to lovingly lead our wives because it is the way of God. We love like He does. And we lead like He does. It is easier for our wives to respect us and submit to us when we are leading from a place of love. God loved us first. In the same way, husbands must love their wives first and then the submission will come. Even if it doesn't come, we would have done what God wanted us to do.

LOVE HER

Chapter 6
HOW DO I LOVE HER?

How do I begin?

Pray and ask God for his wisdom on how to treat his daughter. Keep in mind you are married to the King's daughter. Treat her like she is royalty, and she will act like she is.

Show her the best of your manliness. Open doors for her and pull out her chair. Take her coat. Let her walk on the inside of the street. As much as women scream, they want their independence and equality, they all seem to swoon over chivalrous men. Your wife wants you to treat her like this. It makes her feel special and loved. It disarms her and causes her to let go of her defenses. She feels cherished.

The Lord told me one day in my devotional time. He said,

"Choose to love her one day at a time."

Even though it sounds simple, it was very profound to me. The Lord was showing me that love is not shown only in the bedroom. Neither is it expressed only on birthdays, anniversaries and Valentine's Day. Our wives need more than that. The Lord was teaching me how to love my wife, one 24-hour day at a time.

Lamentations 3:23 They (mercies) are new every morning great is thy faithfulness.

Every day, we as believers are awakened to new mercy extended to us by our loving God. It is like His love is fresh for us. Whatever happened yesterday is locked there. But today is a new day to receive God's love.

It is the same way in a marriage. I don't bring old offenses into a new day, but I look at my wife with fresh eyes. I love her, today. Whatever happened yesterday is buried in the past. So every day I must look for fresh ways to love on her. What she needs today from me may be very different from yesterday or even tomorrow.

Every day that she and I are allowed more time on the earth is another opportunity for me to love on her.

Whatever she needs, God will allow me to supply to her when I am sensitive to Him.

Today, she may need for me to listen to her. Tomorrow, she may need words of encouragement from me. The next day she may need a wrapped gift from me. The following day she may need for me to hold her or watch some movies with her.

I hope you are getting the picture that we are to take special care of our gift by extending love to her every single day, without getting stuck in the same routine.

Jesus washed the feet of the disciples which was an act of service, humility and love. The leader served. Foot washing was an act of hospitality for those who had journeyed. I think that we can draw from the example of Jesus. As the word says, But he that is greatest among you shall be your servant. Matthew 23:11 (KJV).

The head or leader is the one who serves the most. Our service is the way we express our love. We can do little things to brighten our wives' day. I love making my wife tea, not for her health's sake but because it's a simple way that I can express love to her. I love to make it in the mornings and bring it to her while she's in bed. It is the perfect time to tell her how beautiful she is and what a gift she is to me. I enjoy loving my wife, and this is a simple way to do that.

Not only do I love bringing my wife tea in the mornings. But I love sitting with her to watch movies. I love buying her gifts and surprising her with getaways. I love protecting her and watching over her. I love praying for her; I love being there for her as a sounding board when she just needs to vent. Whatever my wife needs, I want to be the one who gives it to her.

You see when you cherish your wife and the gift that she is, God will give you little rituals or things to do based on her love language that would enhance your marriage and help her realize how loved she is. And God gets the glory.

If you don't get anything else from this book, I hope you understand that love is an action word. You can't just tell her you love her, even though you need to do that, too. But you must act on what you say. Make a choice to demonstrate that love to her, daily.

Each little act of love fills her emotional love bank. Your wife needs those little deposits of love even more than the grand gestures. Sure, she wants big gestures, as well. But those little acts of love go a whole lot further because you are depositing into her regularly.

Some men think that because they married their wives, work, and come home every night that this is enough. That's their declaration of love. That's where they miss it. Women are built differently. They need love expressed every day. To the same level that we need respect, they need love. It's not one and done. Men want and need respect every single day.

When God told us to love our wives as Christ loved the church, He did not intend for us to do that in our own strength. But He promises to give us everything we need as husbands if we turn to Him and seek Him for his wisdom.

Keep her first above all others. You need to do this in your thoughts and your actions. There are so many things that are vying for your attention. But outside of God, no one else should have your attention more than your wife. Think of her good qualities. Think about her strengths and the different ways she blesses you. If you spend too much time thinking about her flaws, you won't give her the best part of you.

Proverbs 23:7a reads, As a man thinketh in his heart, so is he. It is true. We act according to what we think. Our behavior is connected to our thoughts. So we must guard our thoughts. Reject negative thoughts of your wife. They come from the enemy. He is always trying to break down your relationship. Think highly of her, and you will treat her in a way that honors God.

And finally, tell her that you love her often. It doesn't have to be cliché'-ish. Say it in different ways.

"I'm glad I married you."

"I don't know where my life would be without you in it."

"You are an amazing wife!"

"I'm so glad I get to spend forever with you."

"You make me happy."

"I love spending time with you."

"I love the way you think."

"My life is full because of you."

Psalms 139:17 says How precious also is thy thoughts unto me, O God how great is the sum of them.

Chapter 7
SECURE HER

Wives need security. It is a man's right and honor to protect his wife. And she wants to know that he will keep her safe and take care of her. God has made us the protectors of our homes. Just as a lion watches over his pride to guard against enemy interference, so must we as the leaders of our homes, watch over our wives and children. God put this instinct in us. There are many outside forces to guard against.

From Me?

But one of the primary persons we need to protect her from is ourselves. As her protector, if you are not careful you can do more damage to her than anyone else. Those that are closest to us, who love us the most are the ones who can hurt us the deepest.

In what ways would a husband need to protect his wife from himself? Well there are four ways. First, you can injure her by being very critical, harsh, and demeaning. Therefore we have to watch not only our words but our tones. Colossians 3:19 (KJV) says, Husbands love your wives and be not bitter against them. Bitterness in the heart makes the words turn sour. Check your heart and watch your tone. Turn the volume down on your dialogue. There is no need to yell. Do you criticize her a lot? Do you put her down or dismiss her? What is your overall attitude towards your wife? If you aren't sure, check with her. What good is it to protect her from others if you are the one trampling all over her heart?

Secondly, we can do damage to her when we seek to protect our own image over her heart. There are times that we may be dishonest, lacking in integrity in a situation to protect our pride. In those times, we are making provision for our flesh and neglecting our duty to cover our wives. Lies and inconsistency injure our wives more than we may be willing to admit. When you are dishonest, you unwittingly push her outside of your trust circle. And she feels like you don't trust her with your truth. Which makes her not trust you. It's an unproductive cycle. It keeps your marriage on the edge of breakdown. Move away from the edge by being honest and transparent. Wherefore put away lying speak every man (husband) by speaking truth with his neighbor (wife): for we are members one of another. Ephesians 4:25 KJV (emphasis mine).

Thirdly, risky behaviors make her vulnerable to insecurity. Husbands who actively live in sin cause their wives to be insecure. Sleeping with other women, embezzlement, selling drugs are types of risky behaviors that leave your family vulnerable to disease, loss, and harm.

However it's not just the obvious sins that affect your wife. Even little questionable behaviors also shake your wife's foundation. These behaviors include driving with an expired license or no auto insurance, leaving underage children alone to run some errand, living without life or health insurance, lying on your income taxes. Risky behaviors can leave her defenseless.

Husbands who take risks expose their wives and families to danger or loss. It is wise to consider the full consequences of a situation before acting. It adversely affects your wife and children Your sin nature wants to do things your way by putting yourself first above all others. It is not responsible and not godly behavior.

God gave us wives and asked us to cover them and take care of them. Our whole life has to change when we take on a family. We must consider what is in the best interest of our wives and children. We have the power to resist temptation and put our wives' need for protection first.

Finally, poor financial stewardship can cause your wife to feel insecure. If you are spending haphazardly with no financial plan in place, you are putting your family in jeopardy. Women tend to have more anxiety when there is not enough money to meet the needs of the family. She wants to know that her future is secure with you. It makes her feel better when you have made provisions for the future, i.e. retirement plans, life insurance, etc. You cannot only be concerned about the present. You must make preparation for the future of your family. If you are unemployed this will make matters worse for her. Prayerfully seek gainful employment. And manage well the finances that God has entrusted to you. That may mean taking a class or two. It could require that you seek wisdom from a financial mentor. But learn how to better manage what you have. It really doesn't matter how much money you make if you are a good steward. I have counseled a couple making 30k annually who had more in savings and investments than another couple making 6 figures. Don't get caught up in the amount you make. Protect your family by being a better steward. Secure your family's financial future. These are the areas that you can address personally.

When you address these 4 areas, it solidifies her security and your marriage will grow There are still other threats to her safety outside of you.

Her In-laws

Your extended family, as wonderful as they may be, are also an external threat to her security. Many times families have a hard time adjusting to new marriages. They resist change and so they reject the person they think responsible for that change – your spouse. However it is important that you draw clear lines in your family. No one is to disregard or disrespect your wife. She takes priority over all other familial relationships.

Your family should not be able to trump a decision she makes or say anything to harm her spirit. She is a part of you and you can't allow them to bring division to your relationship.

Your parents, siblings, children, friends, etc. should understand the importance that you place on your relationship with your wife. If they don't understand, it's your job to help them. Set clear boundaries and make your expectations well-defined.

Husbands, you must be brave enough to speak up to confront those that set themselves up against her. You don't have to be rude, but you should be firm, letting your family know that disrespect to your wife will not be tolerated under any circumstance. It is your job as the family leader to insist that everybody respects her and her place as your wife and God's daughter.

Her family

Sometimes her own family of origin will come against her. Jealousy and unresolved conflicts can hide in families and emerge to chip away at the bit. In these matters, you will have to be delicate and handle them with wisdom. Nevertheless you are still responsible for protecting her. If it becomes necessary to address her family members, make sure you involve her in your strategy. Never disregard your wife's feelings by taking over, without her involvement. She knows her family much better than you. Seek her wise input in how to handle a particular family member.

Protecting her doesn't mean that you have to be mean to people. You can be a gentle giant while making sure your wife is well covered. This doesn't make you weak. It makes you a man she can admire and trust.

Meekness is strength under control. Thus there is no weakness in meekness. It honors God and helps build character in us. God wants you to protect your wife from a place of love -not a place of anger or fear.

Others

It's not always family that will compromise your wife's security. There are rude service people, demeaning medical people, challenging co-workers, arrogant bosses, and the list goes on. Step up to shield her when it's appropriate. An attack on your family is an attack against you. So don't sit silently by. Speak up to protect her.

If others send your wife home broken and in tears, you must stand up for her in a way that honors both the Lord and your wife.

That means we don't have to fight every single battle that arises. Most situations are just irritants and annoyances. Some of those trials are for her growth and spiritual development. Your response is to just be empathetic and compassionate. Listen to her, console her, and pray for her.

Just as there is a time to stand up for your wife, there is also a time to stand down. There may be times that you may want to roar but God or your wife says no. You will have to resist the urge to act or react. Be prayerful and patient. Let the Lord give you peace. Humility and quietness could be what God wants to develop in you.

The Bible instructs us to be angry but without sin. So anger is a natural human reaction, but learn to handle it with wisdom. Resist the urge to get revenge. I know this is easier said than done, but God will help us if we ask him to. Walk in forgiveness.

I had to learn this the hard way. Sometimes I would hastily say the wrong thing. Or sometimes I didn't say anything at all. Eventually, I learned to be led by the Spirit. The Lord teaches us when to be the lion and when to be the lamb.

There is a time to roar and time to be gentle. We must discern the right times. As you develop your own relationship with the Lord, you will perceive what should be done. All things lawful are not expedient (I Corinthians 10:23 KJV). That means just because you have the right to do something doesn't mean you should do it. The method or the timing may not be right for that situation.

There are some other practical ways we can protect our wives to make her feel secure.

Be the first in the house: Don't send your wife in an empty house first, especially if you have been away from home for an extended period of time. You don't want her to surprise an intruder. This helps her feel you are concerned about her well-being.

Don't send her out at night by herself. If she needs to go to the store, you should go instead or wait until the morning. There are all types of evil people waiting to take advantage of women who are alone, especially at night. Be wise. Cover her and your children.

Always walk on the outside on the sidewalk, never put her closer to the passing cars. If a car veers off the path, you will be able to block her from being hit.

Don't allow her to pump the gas while you sit in the car and don't send her in store while you wait outside. This not only looks bad, it transfers the burden of leadership on the wife instead of the husband. Remember the leader is the one who serves most.

Don't allow her to carry heavy packages or weighty luggage. Carry it for her. You are her strength.

Do all that is in your power to keep your bride secure. She will measure that as love. And a wife that feels loved will certainly respond to her husband much more enthusiastically than one who doesn't.

Mr. Don't Fix it

Your wife will have different types of struggles. And in those times, her security is in your presence. Wives may struggle with a friendship, her body changes, a diminished self-image, etc.. When she comes to share her troubles with you, should not try to fix it by offering a solution, unless she asks for it.

It is the tendency of most men to try to problem solve instead of dealing with an issue. It's our default. We like to take the short cut by giving a quick fix. This keeps us from having to deal with the emotions of the situation. An emotional woman tends to make us feel a tad bit uncomfortable. We want to hurry her over this "thing" she's dealing with. That's a little selfish on our parts. Instead of trying to fix it, let's enter into our wives' emotions by letting her get through her process. Pray with her and find ways to empathize with her. A little compassion and patience can go a long way to making her feel secure.

Seek to connect with your wife emotionally at whatever level she is. Ask questions for understanding. It allows you to get a grip on what's really going on. Then you can enter into her pain and emotions.

Remember, as men, when we try to 'fix it', we are avoiding the painful situation or trauma. Don't push it away. Draw into it with her. You will find yourself more intimate. Let God lead the way.

Chapter 8
SEX

———————⊃○⊂———————

Sex is a good and healthy expression of love between a man and his wife. It was birth from the heart and mind of God and gifted to the couple on the first day of their union. It is the glue that connects a husband to his bride. We know sex is important to us. But we have to know it is also important to God. So how does a man love his wife sexually in a way that pleases God?

Men and women have different approaches to sex. I'm sure you have heard that men are like microwaves and women are like slow cookers or some other similar comparison.

When it comes to sex, men have a more physical approach, while women approach sex from a more emotional standpoint He responds by sight, and she responds by feeling. But these differences are meant to complement us, not create tension.

In his prime, a man is almost always ready for sex. It takes a lot more priming for a woman to warm up. She will need to connect with her husband, first. If she doesn't sense that connection, she may feel used. Loving her requires that a husband slow down enough to engage with his wife. He should not limit his approach to when they are in bed. A wife wants to feel loved before she gets to bed.

One of the ways to express love to her is to approach her with thoughtfulness. What does she want, and how is she feeling? Or what does she need? These are all good questions to ask yourself. The main point is to avoid making sex all about you.

Most women want to satisfy their husbands sexually. And many tend to ignore their needs to meet his. Husbands can sometimes be more self-centered and look to sex for their own pleasure, without thought of what their wives' needs are.

If you are focused on your own satisfaction, then your wife will be neglected in this area. If she's focused on you, and you are focused on you; then, no one is focused on her. To approach sex in a way that pleases God, we must take a more *selfless* attitude.

In the ideal marriage, the wife seeks to please her husband, and the husband seeks to please his wife. That means you will need to pay attention to her and talk to her to know how to please her.

It is the lazy husband who just does what he's always done. Just because something worked in the past doesn't mean that it will work going forward. Women change. What they liked one day will not be what they want/need the next. Remember that God said love her one day at a time. Today is a new day approach it as such. Otherwise, you both may find yourselves disappointed and unfulfilled.

The scripture says that the husband's body belongs to his wife, and the wife's body belongs to her husband (1 Corinthians 7:4). However that does not give the husband a right to demand sex from his wife. He shouldn't force her or try to coerce her to give in to his pressures. The wise husband woos his wife. He invites her. He does not abuse the gift that God has granted him.

Marriages go through seasons, which also affects the sexual relationship. So be sensitive to her. If she is struggling through pre-menopause/menopause or some physical ailment, don't get angry or frustrated. She needs your understanding. Read up on the health condition so you can understand what she is going through and support her. There is more to marriage than just sex. So show that you care about her overall well-being.

Sexual frequency may wane. That doesn't mean you give up on your relationship. Pray for your sexual connection and continue working at it to make it enjoyable for you both.

Keep your sexual relationship pure and holy before God. That means you should not bring others into your bedroom, literally or figuratively. Figuratively means visualizing another woman while you are having sex with your wife (images from porn or fantasies). Another woman in your bed is a violation of God's law, and it will jeopardize your marriage. So don't cheat on your wife or offer to bring a third party in your bed. You will find yourself down a slippery slope that will be hard to recover from.

LOVE HER

I stepped outside of my marriage at one point, but thank
God for his mercy and my wife for her forgiveness. We
were able to recover, and I never ventured down that road
ever again. I did like Job and made a covenant with my
eyes to not look lustfully on another woman.

Adultery can cause your whole world to come crashing
down. I've seen many men lose everything because they
chose to continue down the path of adultery. The enemy
wound up cheating them out of their relationship with God
and their families. They were left with nothing. Men often
don't consider that when they cheat on their wives, they are
also cheating on their children. The children feel the brunt
of that betrayal, and it can create a breach in their
relationship forever.

Hebrews 13:4 says Marriage is honorable in all, and the
bed undefiled: but whoremongers and adulterers God will
judge. So be vigilant. No matter how tempting, guard your

marriage from adultery. If you take fire in your bosom you will be burned (Proverbs 6:27). So be cautious. The enemy wants to destroy you and your family. Seek out an accountability partner to help you stay on the straight and narrow path.

Equally damaging is bringing pornography in your marriage. Whether it's movies, online images, or magazines, they all can wreck your marriage. The Bible says that lust is never satisfied. Please know that you will find yourself deeper than you ever intended to go. Pornography takes the attention off your wife and causes you to become more internal. It allows you to escape into a fantasy world of sin. This creates a disconnection between not just you and your wife, but you and your God.

So while you may be physical with your wife, you are not intimate with her. And many times, she feels it. Even if you are able to deceive your wife, you can never fool God. He sees. Proverbs 6:32-33 reads, *But* whoso committeth adultery with a woman lacketh understanding: he *that* doeth it destroyeth his own soul. His word says the reproach of the adulterer is never wiped away. A wound and dishonour shall he get; and his reproach shall not be wiped away.

Even after you may have stopped viewing the porn, the images are still imbedded in your mind. You will have to seek God for deliverance.

Pure sexual intimacy begins with her heart. Smart husbands start there before they get to the ministry of the body. Encourage her, forgive her, speak words of affirmation, make her feel wanted and loved.

Don't just be ready to jump into the act. Lead up to it. This will make her feel appreciated and will definitely enhance your sex life.

Love your wife's body. Speak well of it. Women tend to struggle in this area. So affirm her body. And be appreciative by saying, thank you.

Healthy sex requires a peaceful and relaxed mindset at atmosphere. Deal with your stress in prayer. Give every trouble over to the Lord and settle your differences with your wife before you approach her for sex. You must minister to her heart before you can minister to her body. And if her heart is broken or wounded by something you have said or done, it is insensitive of you to just expect her to yield her body. She may render her body, but her heart will be far away from you. Love puts in the effort to make sure she is okay.

Eliminate distractions. Turn off your cell phone and television. Give her your full attention. If you have children, make sure you have a lock on your bedroom door.

Healthy sex does not equal wonderful, exhilarating sex all of the time. Sex can be amazing, but the reality is that it isn't every single time. And that's okay. Keep working to make it better for the both of you. But don't let your ego tell you that your wife must have an orgasm each time. You will put undue pressure on yourself and your wife. Just relax and enjoy pleasuring her. Women can enjoy the experience with or without an orgasm. Talk to her about what she wants. She may be surprised that you are interested, but she will give you the information you seek.

She may want sex when you don't. Don't just shut her down. Let her stir you up. Be open to pleasuring her.

Couples have to work at their sexual relationship to keep it strong and vibrant. That means making it a priority.

Keep adjusting to keep connecting. If sex becomes difficult, don't give up. In the same way, you don't give up when finances are tight. You keep working until you find something that works.

Sex is meant to be a lot of things, and I can't help but think fun is one of them. So enjoy your sex life, love each other and laugh together. And always remember to give God the glory for your wife.

LOVE HER

Chapter 9
ROMANCE

There is nothing a wife desires more than a sensitive, romantic husband. Unfortunately, husbands tend to scoff at romance. Men can misunderstand romance. They tend to feel like romance is somehow feminine; and it's not something that men should do. However, the opposite is true. The greatest romantic of all time is Jesus Christ.

The passion of Christ is His bride. She is his heartthrob. He was so wildly in love with her that He was willing to die for that love. And He did.

We can see many romantic gestures of God towards His bride:

He has written her name in the palm of hands. (Isaiah 49:16)

He thinks about her so much that the number of thoughts is more than the grains of sand on the seashore. (Psalms 139:18)

He holds her hand in His. (Isaiah 41:13)

He loves her with an everlasting love. (Jeremiah 31:3)

We serve a romantic God. He is in love with his bride and is constantly wooing us to himself. (Luke 19:10)

Your wife wants your attention, and she wants to be pursued by you. You pursued her to win her heart to get her to marry you. But it doesn't stop at "I do." Your continuous pursuit of her is what romance is all about.

Romance is neither feminine or masculine. It's gender neutral but should be practiced by both men and women. Romance is the lengths that a man or woman will go to demonstrate love for the other. Most people want to be romanced, including men. Even though most men probably won't admit it; because of his limited understanding of the word.

For us as men, romance is not flowers and candy or candlelight dinners. Romance is foot rubs, watching the game with his wife, or his wife serving him breakfast in bed. It's the same idea. You want her to sacrifice for you. That is what romance is all about.

And if you are going to love your wife, you must be willing to romance her. She wants to know that you will go beyond the ordinary to love on her. Romance doesn't start with sex, but it can certainly end there.

She may love getting flowers sent to her job or a surprise gift every so often.

Chocolates and flowers are definitely in the romantic category. However, you must know that she likes those things. Otherwise, it is not romantic for her.

The gift or gesture you offer to your spouse must show her that you are thinking about her and that she means the world to you. That usually won't include any gifts that are chore related: irons, toasters, vacuum cleaners, pruning shears, etc.

It's also important that you don't copy something you've seen someone else do for their wife. Your wife may not like that gesture. Be creative. Pray. Listen to her. Study your wife to know what will wow her.

Sometimes I plan a picnic in our bedroom, a romantic candlelight bath, or get my wife tickets to a play or ballet.

My wife loves the arts. So I encourage that part of her. I've also taken her on countless trips.

Surprise!

The surprise element will add to whatever romantic gesture you are planning. It's the icing on the cake. I've planned a surprise shopping trip to Galveston, TX. I had my son act like he wanted to take us out, and then made an excuse to stop by the airport. When we got to the airport, my wife was in awe when I already had her suitcase packed in the back of the car and handed her a card with cash in it for a surprise shopping trip.

Actively do those little things that will ignite romance in your marriage. God is always doing things for us to demonstrate his love. Think about how God loves you on a daily basis. Get inspiration from Him.

Some men are romantics at heart, although it takes a little more effort for others. When we hear the word, we tend to shrink back, thinking our gestures have to be grandiose. You know, the blimp with skywriting or an expensive destination trip. The reality is romance is not at all that complicated. The big gestures are great. But realistically, not everyone has a budget for that. As long as you are consistently showing romance to your wife, you are good. Romance is not about spending your life's savings; It's not defined by the big gestures. In fact, romance doesn't even have to have a cost associated with it. Romance is all about doing little things for your wife on a regular basis that show her you are willing to go the extra mile. That's what she wants. She wants to know she is worth the extra effort. Display your love in a way that convinces her that she is the most important person in the world to you.

The best way to keep romance as an important part of your marriage is to keep up with your date nights. She should not be the only one interested in your date nights. In some marriages, if the wife doesn't plan date night, the couple would never go out. That is unfortunate because the marriage will suffer. The husband is the head of the family. He should set the tone for the marriage. It's not solely his wife's job to plan dates.

Once a week set aside time for just the two of you. If you can't find a babysitter, be creative. Let the kids do something fun (watch movies, play games, etc.) if they are younger, put them to bed earlier.

Dating your wife causes you to look for new ways to romance her. Dating her keeps the fire burning in your relationship. Your marriage doesn't become dull and routine. Dating energizes you both, and it keeps the marriage fresh.

Once you have the mindset of dating your wife, it will help you to remember to do little things to keep the romance going on a regular basis.

You would be wise not to let the romance fade in your relationship. Our wives need and deserve our continued adoration, thoughtfulness, and love. Give her your very best each and every day.

Don't allow yourself to get caught up in the busyness of life and take your wife for granted. Your marriage will get stale and dull if you think romance is not required. Your wife deserves your continual pursuit.

I have studied my wife's love language. It is gifts and words of affirmation. So in order to continually romance her, I surprise her with gifts. She can be sitting at the computer working, and I will come home with a little gift bag or wrapped gift. Or sometimes I order it so that it comes in the mail. It is at that time that I'm showing her romance.

I also post on social media how much I love her. I do that because her secondary love language is words of affirmation. I build her up both in front of others and behind the scenes. I send her text messages or buy her cards to encourage her.

Some husbands don't even try in the area of romance and their wives suffer as a result. I hope that's not you. If you try to romance your wife, I believe God will bless you in it. He has certainly done that for me.

Cherish every moment you have with her. You just don't know how long you will have with her. None of us will live forever. Many people are living in regret today because they took their spouses for granted. And the spouse died. They wish they would've done things differently or spent more time with him or her. Let's not waste time. Give your spouse the best part of you. Love her. Honor her. Bless her. And you will surely reap all that you have sown.

Below I have listed some ways to romance your wife. It will require that you know her well. Some of these will work for her, and some will not. But I hope that these can be a springboard for some better ideas:

- Surprise her with treats or gifts, just because.
- Watch her favorite movies with her.
- Prepare a candlelight dinner for just the two of you.
- Put rose petals on the bed and give her a card.
- Sing to her on social media.
- Take her somewhere she has always wanted to go.
- Send flowers or singing telegram to her job.
- Cuddle with her by the fireplace.
- Give her maid service for a day.
- Write her love notes and paste them on her mirror.

- Compose a playlist of romantic songs

- Ask her to marry you again

- Take her on a horse and carriage ride.

- Wash/rub her feet

- Compose a song for her

- Bring a picnic lunch to her job

- Write her a poem

- Upgrade her ring

- Paint her toenails

- Take her dreaming in a nicer neighborhood

- Send her a letter/card through the mail

- Give her a day at the spa

- Take a late evening walk while holding her hand.

LOVE HER

Chapter 10
WE NEED TO TALK

———————————⊃∘⊂———————————

Why do we cringe when we hear those words? Our wives seem always to want to talk to us. And usually, it's not about something positive. There is usually a problem in you or the marriage that she wants to address. Our natural tendency as men is to avoid problems. We don't want to hear about how we have failed or missed something. But maturity requires that we don't go with what is our natural tendency, but we should lean into the spiritual.

When I was a child, I spoke as a child. But when I became a man, I put childish things behind me 1 Corinthians 13:11. Maturity requires that I speak and deal differently with my wife. That means I am open to discuss adult issues to bring resolution.

This is an important area in all marriages. We have to learn to do better in loving our wives is in our communication. We have to speak and listen as men.

Sometimes I still struggle with communicating effectively with my wife. But I have grown a lot over the years, and I am still working on myself and growing into who God wants me to be.

Communication is an art that must be perfected on purpose. None of us have arrived. As long as we are on this earth, there will always be room for growth. So be open to working on your listening and speaking skills.

There are six areas that we, as men, have as a common struggle. I want to deal with those primary behavior areas that cause us to miss communication.

1. We tune her out. Proverbs 5:1 reads, My son attend unto my wisdom and bow thine ear to my understanding. Don't ignore her or pretend to listen while your attention is somewhere else. You will miss part of what is said because you are not really interested. When she doesn't feel heard, she also doesn't feel valued or loved. When we listen, we allow our wives to share their hearts. We don't always have to talk, and again we don't always have to fix it. Sometimes we just need to listen. Let her tell you what she thinks, even if you can barely stand to hear it. This could be a place for your marriage to grow. Listen with an open mind in a calm manner while she explains what she needs from you. You are giving yourself to her, and this is part of the price. I know it can be difficult to listen to criticism, but your

marriage needs this in order to move forward. Not just for your marriage but also for your wife.

2. We are too offensive. Change your tone. Sometimes if we are passionate about a subject, we can come off as loud or rude. This can shut her down or cause an argument to ensue. Sarcasm, over-talking her or yelling can create a lot of conflict within the relationship. Be sensitive to her. Remember, a *disagreement does not have to equal an argument.* Having a disagreement with your spouse is not abnormal. Certainly you can agree to disagree without being enraged. Calmly, state your position. Ask questions for clarity, but there really is no reason to be angry.

3. We listen to respond. Don't just listen to give a clever comeback. That's not real communication. It may feel like you are just trying to win an argument. Remember, you are a team. You are on the same side. If one of you wins, the marriage loses.

Hear her heart more than her words or attitude. Again ask questions for clarity of message. Sometimes emotions can block the real message. Be willing to hear correction and grow. Seek to progress in your verbal exchange. The goal is to reach some resolution that benefits your relationship.

4. We go silent. Don't give her the silent treatment. Remember, we put away immature behavior. Real men have a voice. It's better to tell her what the issue is instead of allowing the enemy to minister something totally different to her heart. Giving your wife the cold shoulder is disrespectful and doesn't show love. If you feel too angry to speak, tell her that. Then take a moment to pray. You should come back ready to communicate effectively with your wife.

5. We don't say what we really want to say. Say what you really mean. Don't say one thing and mean something different. And don't just tell her what you think she wants to hear to avoid conflict. How can your marriage grow if you are not honest? If there is something you don't like,

speak up. Your wife really wants to hear your heart. Even though there may be times, she resists. She still wants to know your true heart. It is unproductive to tell her you want one thing when you really want something else. That undermines your relationship. Be fair and share.

6. We get defensive. When it's time to talk, don't come ready to fight. Some men attack their wives because she brings up some area that they need to grow in. Others divert the conversation to all the things they have done "right". If she has a complaint in one area (i.e. finances) that doesn't mean she is devaluing what you've done in other areas (i.e. chores). Mature leaders can take correction, process it, and grow from it. When your wife says she wants to talk she is saying she wants you both to work to improve the marriage.

Lead her with the behavior that you want her to emulate. Be willing to work on yourself to change and grow. Just like you want her to change and grow.

Give her your full attention when you are talking. Shut down your phone, computer, television, etc. and focus completely on what she is saying. You are less likely to misunderstand if you are completely tuned in.

Communication can be a real struggle. I get it. Sometimes you may not want to hear what your wife has to say. However, it is necessary for our growth. Sometimes the Lord is speaking through her. She will say what most others won't.

The Lord spoke to Abraham and told him to listen to Sara when she put Hagar out.. Pilate's wife had a dream about Jesus, and Pilate listened to his wife and washed his hands of Jesus's blood.

So the next time she says, "We need to talk," respond eagerly, "You're right honey. Let's grow our marriage."

LOVE HER

Chapter 11
YOUR BEST WORK

———————◦———————

We are the priests of our homes. An effective leader must always consult the King of kings. Luke 18:1 says, And he spake a parable unto them *to this end,* that men ought always to pray, and not to faint. Men never underestimate the power of prayer in your marriage and home. How can we lead properly without direction from the Lord?

We are anointed to lead our families. That means keeping Christ at the helm. Pray for and with your wife. She needs your spiritual leadership.

Pray in your own words, but according to God's Word. Eloquent words are not required. And pray for as short or as long as you feel led. A 5-minute prayer could be just as effective as an hour long prayer. The most important thing about prayer is that do it.

This is a prayer I pray for my wife and my marriage.

A Husband's Prayer
Oh Lord, I lift to you the most amazing gift given to me in this life, my precious wife. May I always love her, cherish her and nurture her.

Forgive me for those times I have neglected her and taken her for granted.

Lord, fill my mouth with praise for her instead of complaint and criticism. Help me to talk to her when I don't feel like it and share my intimate feelings with her. Help me to love her like you loved the church by dying to my own selfish needs and desires. And remind me to always keep her in first position right behind you.

May I never abuse my authority as her head. Teach me how to lovingly lead her back to you and never to myself. May I always pastor her, protect her, and provide for her according to your will.

Lord, this is my wife, you have created her for me. Let my love cover her sins and heal her brokenness. May I encourage her in her own gifts and talents and never be threatened by her abilities.

As we are on this journey together, may I never leave her feeling alone but always comforted by my love. And as we look back, may we never regret the journey, but enjoy it until we get home.

In Jesus's name, I pray. Amen.

LOVE HER

About the Author

Oscar Jones is the co-founder of Marriage For A Lifetime Ministries, along with his beautiful wife of 38 years, Crystal. The two have a passion for marriage ministry. Oscar has written 3 books for men and co-authored several books with his wife and ministry partner. He also leads the Restore the Roar Men's Ministry, hosting rallies and conferences all over the country. He lives with his wife in the Atlanta area. They have 5 adult children, two in-laws and 9 grandchildren.